For:

. . . .

. . . .

Town&Country

WITHDRAWN

WEDDING VOWS & PROMISES

CAROLINE TIGER

HEARST BOOKS

A division of Sterling Publishing Co., Inc.

New York / London

www.sterlingpublishing.com

Copyright ©2008 by Sterling Publishing Co., Inc.

Library of Congress Cataloging-in-Publication Data
Tiger, Caroline.
  Town & country : wedding vows & promises / Caroline Tiger.
      p. cm.
  Includes index.
  ISBN-13: 978-1-58816-618-0
  ISBN-10: 1-58816-618-X
  1. Marriage service. 2. Weddings—Planning. I. Town & country. II. Title.
III. Title: Town and country.
  HQ745.T54 2007
  395.2'2--dc22

                                                                2006038512

10 9 8 7 6 5 4 3 2 1

Book design by Barbara Balch
Illustrations by Ann Boyajian

Published by Hearst Books
A Division of Sterling Publishing Co., Inc.
387 Park Avenue South, New York, NY 10016

Town & Country and *Hearst Books* are trademarks of
Hearst Communications, Inc.

www.townandcountrymag.com

For information about custom editions, special sales, premium and
corporate purchases, please contact Sterling Special Sales Department
at 800-805-5489 or *specialsales@sterlingpub.com*.

Distributed in Canada by Sterling Publishing
c/o Canadian Manda Group, 165 Dufferin Street
Toronto, Ontario, Canada M6K 3H6

Distributed in Australia by Capricorn Link (Australia) Pty. Ltd.
P.O. Box 704, Windsor, NSW 2756 Australia

Manufactured in China

Sterling ISBN 13: 978-1-58816-618-0
          ISBN 10: 1-58816-618-X

CONTENTS

FOREWORD

My husband, who once seemed destined for life-long bachelorhood, always contends that the most meaningful part of our wedding day was the exchanging of vows during the ceremony. That moment, according to him, sealed the relationship. We have now been married for a quarter of a century. Looking back on that fateful day, I have to agree with the groom. There was something about that moment that created a deep bond between us.

Certainly it had to do with the setting: a candlelit ceremony in a beautiful Episcopalian cathedral. Having it presided over by a young female minister who had never before joined a couple in matrimony—we were her first victims—also added immensely to the occasion. She had a clear, confident voice and a lovely, approving smile. Then there were the vows themselves. I could go on but to do so would be to invade my own privacy and that of my husband. Suffice it to say that I remember every second.

> *BECAUSE I LOVE YOU TRULY,*
> *BECAUSE YOU LOVE ME, TOO,*
> *MY VERY GREATEST HAPPINESS*
> *IS SHARING LIFE WITH YOU.*

Our wedding took place in 1982, well before I became editor in chief of *Town & Country*. When I arrived at the magazine in 1993, I realized that our weddings pages were among our most popular. *Town & Country*, by the way, was founded in 1846, so our coverage of weddings dates back to pre–Civil War days. And while almost everything has changed since that time of horse-and-buggy transportation (also, an era of no telephones or indoor plumbing, not to mention airplanes or computers), weddings are one of the rare occasions that still adhere to certain long-held traditions and rules of etiquette.

Granted, the traditions are fewer, and the rules are far less strict than they used to be. But it's quite extraordinary when you think about it: the bride still wears a long white gown and walks down the aisle, accompanied by her father or closest male member of the family. There is a protocol to be followed regarding where friends and family of the bride and groom are seated during the service. It is an event that usually requires months of planning and great attention to detail (unless, that is, you plan to elope—in which case you have no need for this book).

If, however, the idea of going through the many steps that lead to the altar is something you have dreamed of all of your life, then this guide is definitely one that will help you get prepared and organized. It will also help family members and those in the wedding party.

Above all, remember that this is your wedding and no one else's. As bride and groom, you have the opportunity to create a day that is uniquely your own. As the saying goes, "If love makes the world go 'round, then you make it spin." The same applies to your wedding day.

—Pamela Fiori, Editor in Chief,
Town & Country

INTRODUCTION

ALL BRIDES AND GROOMS know they must make certain decisions early in the wedding-planning process: these include ceremony and reception venue, length of guest list and wedding colors. After cementing these key factors, more concerns tumble into view: gown, flowers, bridesmaids' dresses, table settings, cake, favors, seating charts—the list goes on and on. But where are the words? Until it's time to write the invitations, they often remain an afterthought. Ignored and discounted, quotidian words don't come into play until someone makes an emergency dash to the bookstore to pore through etiquette books on a quest for how to address an invitation to an army lieutenant who's married to a superior court judge. It's just not right. We implore you: give words their proper due. You won't be sorry. When chosen well and in concert with your personal wedding style, they go further than any other detail in setting the tone.

A Few Words on Etiquette

THOUGH PERSONALIZING your wedding materials is encouraged, the advice in these pages nods first and foremost to tradition and etiquette. There are several reasons. A wedding involves two families coming together, and within those families there are guaranteed to be many different personalities and long-standing and possibly different ways of communicating. Treading lightly and squarely along a prescribed path is one way to avoid conflict during the months leading up to the wedding. Most of the time people can agree on the "right thing" even if it's not "their thing."

Second, etiquette eases the way for guests. When there are set rules to follow, they won't worry about details such as how to RSVP, what to wear, whom to bring and what to give as a gift. Without these worries, everyone can direct their full attention to celebrating your unique and special union.

How To Use This Book

VISUALLY, YOUR WEDDING MATERIALS share unifying features: consistency in colors, possibly a logo, such as a monogram of your initials entwined. The same should be true of your choice of words. How will you announce, both orally and in writing, your engagement? How will you word your save-the-date cards? Will you create a wedding website? For the ceremony itself, which words define you? What lyrics, novels, poems and quotations move you? Which have meaning for your relationship? From setting the right first impression to memorializing your wedding after the fact, this book will guide you in choosing what's right for you from beginning to end.

The chapters are arranged chronologically, but you're encouraged to skip around and dip in and out as need dictates. For example, you may want to coordinate the words on your favors with the words on your invitations. Look for inspiration in the quotations throughout and in the pages of suggested vows and readings. Jot down ideas in the notes pages at the end. You never know when the perfect idea for a clever ring engraving might pop into your head; keep this book close by.

Chapter One

PROPOSALS

A new life begins with just one question. The proposal sets everything in motion. And even if the proposal is no surprise—even if a bride and groom have discussed marriage at length and gone shopping together for a ring—a formal proposal is necessary. In this case, "formal" doesn't mean a black-tie evening accompanied by a string quartet (there's enough time for that later). Simply, a proposal should register as an event—a well-planned series of steps that shows sincere thought and sweet romance.

ASKING FATHER'S PERMISSION

THE OLD-FASHIONED GROOM-TO-BE will want to secure his bride's father's permission before he pops the question. This custom dates back to a time when a daughter was considered her father's property, and the request for permission was literal. If the groom-to-be didn't sanction the father's nod, he was plum out of luck. The father had the power to release his daughter for marriage—or not. Imagine!

In the twenty-first century, approaching the bride's father is not necessary, but it's a much-recommended gesture of respect. Like most modern adaptations of out-moded traditions, the actual step-by-step procedure is not clear. Requesting a future father-in-law's blessing can be more anxiety-provoking than proposing marriage. What should you say once you have your bride's father alone? Here are some guidelines:

- Although an in-person discussion is preferable, a telephone call is acceptable if the future father-in-law is outside of one day's travel by car.

- Break away. It is always best to get your future father-in-law away from the rest of the family so you can talk to him privately. This will help set the scene and show the importance of the request that you're making.

> *MUSIC I HEARD WITH YOU*
> *WAS MORE THAN MUSIC;*
> *AND BREAD I BROKE WITH YOU*
> *WAS MORE THAN BREAD.*
> —ANONYMOUS

- Once you have his undivided attention, indicate that you're opening up a line of serious conversation. You may want to say something along the lines of: "Mr. Smith, there's a reason I asked you to come for a walk with me. I'd like to talk with you about something very important."

- Keep it simple. There's no need for poetry or flowery language. All a father wants to hear is that you're committed to loving his daughter for the rest of your life. You may want to begin with a statement that can't be denied: "Sir, I love your daughter very much." Or show your respect with a little flattery: "Sir, I bow to your parenting skills. You've raised the perfect woman."

- Close the deal. This is the point when you state why you're there: "Sir, what I'm trying to say is that I am planning on asking your daughter to marry me, but before I do so, I'd like your blessing."

> *A SUCCESSFUL MARRIAGE REQUIRES*
> *FALLING IN LOVE MANY TIMES,*
> *ALWAYS WITH THE SAME PERSON.*
> —*MIGNON MCLAUGHLIN*

PROPOSING MARRIAGE

THINGS WERE SO MUCH EASIER in the nineteenth century when a declaration of love was tantamount to a proposal. Then again, courtship and wooing were subject to many more rules back then, so maybe modern-day couples are the ones who have it easy. Whatever your perspective, if you want to get married, there's no getting around the proposal.

There are many factors to take into account when deciding on the perfect way to propose to the one you love. The setting, the words, the character of your relationship, the personality of your mate—these are all very important things to think about.

Is your bride a public person? If she is, she may love to be proposed to in front of a stadium full of people at a major-league baseball game. If she's more traditional, she may prefer a nice, candlelit dinner at a romantic restaurant. If she's sentimental, she might enjoy a trip down memory lane with visits to places of importance in your past together with a proposal at the end. The main thing you must consider is what she will like.

No matter the location, you should get down on one knee and gaze up at her adoringly. You want to make her feel like the most important person in the world.

As for what you say, it's nice to prepare a few words to explain why you're asking her to marry you. For example, you could say, "You are the love of my life. I want to spend forever by your side. Will you marry me?"

Chapter Two

ENGAGEMENT

After she says "yes," you may both feel the need to broadcast the news to every passing stranger. The instinct is understandable, but it needs to be quashed. Before you hire that sky-writing plane, you should take stock of the specific protocol for how and to whom you should spread the good news.

WHEN AND IN WHAT ORDER?

CONSIDER KEEPING IT TO YOURSELF for at least half a day. Uttering the words "We're engaged" is guaranteed to bring on an avalanche of questions, not to mention demands and unsolicited advice. Don't make

> ## SOMETHING OLD,
> ### SOMETHING NEW,
> ### SOMETHING BORROWED,
> ### SOMETHING BLUE.
> —OLD ENGLISH RHYME

the mistake of blurting out the news; later on you will wish you had waited. When you are ready, here's the order that makes the most sense:

CHILDREN FIRST

Your engagement is very exciting, but you must remember that this union is going to greatly affect the lives of any children in the picture. You must handle the situation carefully—give children advance notice and ample time to get used to the idea of bringing in a new member of the family. You want them to be as comfortable with the situation as possible before spreading the news to a wider audience. Informing the children's other parent, your ex, early on is also advisable.

PARENTS

If there are no kids or ex-husbands or -wives, the traditional order of notification is bride's family, then groom's family. Each set of parents should be told separately. The best-case scenario is to tell each set in person, as a couple. Make an impromptu visit home, or, if they live nearby, invite them to your home.

A private place is best; this is an emotional moment, and people should feel free to express those emotions. Of course, if there's any reason to anticipate that parents will be unenthusiastic, you may want to strategize accordingly and stage the announcement in a public space, and consider sharing the news without your fiancé. If it's not possible to announce the exciting news in person, try to both get on the phone or hand the phone off so both partners have a chance to get in on all of the cries of joy and goodwill.

GRANDPARENTS, SIBLINGS AND OTHER CLOSE RELATIVES

This is the time to flex those diplomacy skills. Whom to tell among close relatives and in what order can be tricky; you may want to consider a family get-together to tell a group all at once. Or you may want to delegate some of these announcements to your parents.

HOW TO TELL EVERYONE ELSE

Try to combine telling your close friends with asking them to be part of your wedding party. Most others will find out

> *I LOVE YOU SO PASSIONATELY,*
> *THAT I HIDE A GREAT PART OF MY LOVE,*
> *NOT TO OPPRESS YOU WITH IT.*
> —*MARIE DE RABUTIN-CHANTAL*

through word of mouth or from an engagement announcement (see below). If there are friends who aren't close enough to be included in the bridal party but who are close enough to have known that a proposal was in the offing, call them on the phone to announce the happy news and to recount the highlights (just a few fun details—nothing too personal, of course). Send a short, playful e-mail announcement to acquaintances and coworkers to relieve their suspense. The bride can send an e-mail to her compatriots and the groom to his. This saves both from parroting the news twenty times a day during the week following their engagement, and it's a cue to guests to shift their focus to awaiting the save-the-dates.

ENGAGEMENT ANNOUNCEMENTS

HISTORICALLY, ANNOUNCEMENTS or "banns" were made to the general public in order to give people a chance to object to the proposed union. Nowadays, this broad announcement is simply to let others know about the marriage rather than to give them a say in whether or not it should occur. Because of this, it's very common to wait until the wedding to announce the news in a newspaper, alumni magazine or any other publication. Some of the more superstitious consider announcing an engagement a potential jinx, especially if you haven't yet set a date. Some other reasons to wait:

- If you're planning a long engagement. (Save yourself from running into people a year after the announcement runs and having to answer questions about why the wedding hasn't yet occurred.)

- If you're a widower or a divorcée, and former family members do not yet know of your plans.

- If a divorce hasn't quite been finalized, so you are technically still married to someone else.

- If you'd like to include a picture of the two of you from the wedding day.

If there is no reason to wait for the announcement, let your parents know. One or both sets of parents may want to run a newspaper announcement in their respective hometown publications and perhaps in other places such as private-club or association newsletters. If your parents are deceased and you would still like an announcement to run in your hometown newspaper, a relative or close friend can submit it on your behalf. For announcements to run in high school or college alumni magazines, the bride and groom are in charge of submissions. For all announcements, double check to make sure duplicates aren't being sent to the same publications.

To begin the submission process, call the editorial office at the publication and ask them about their guidelines, deadlines and, if applicable, fees. Some publications have a boilerplate form they will ask you to fill out. Others will ask for a write-up that is not to exceed a certain number of words. Usually an announcement includes the following information:

- Who's hosting the wedding

- Parents' names and places of residence

- Bride and groom's ages, career and education credentials, place of residence if it's different from those of the parents

- Wedding date, month or season ("A June wedding is planned," or "A fall wedding is planned.")

- Engagement photo (if they run photos)

> # *I LOVE YOU MORE THAN YESTERDAY,*
> ## *LESS THAN TOMORROW.*

The more complex the family situation, the more the wording becomes like figuring out a complicated long-division problem. Here are some samples:

BRIDE'S PARENTS

Mr. and Mrs. Noah Fletcher of Saddle Brook, New Jersey, announce the engagement of their daughter, Kayla Noelle, to Matthew McGuire, son of Michael and Petra McGuire of Cherry Hill, New Jersey. Ms. Fletcher, a graduate of University of Pennsylvania Law School, is an associate at Whiteman, Jones & Kotter, a firm in Scarsdale, New York. Mr. McGuire graduated from St. John's University and is a professor at the City University of New York. A spring wedding is planned.

REMARRIED PARENT

Ms. Gloria Hillford and Mr. Kyle Hillford announce the engagement of Ms. Hillford's daughter, Ms. Jodi Elizabeth Banks, to Mr. Frank Bellows. . . . Ms. Banks is also the daughter of Mr. David Banks of Peoria, Illinois.

Deceased Parents

Ms. Jill Batcheller announces the engagement of Ms. Robin Margaret Altman, daughter of the late Mr. Duane Altman and Ms. Gloria Altman, to Mr. Jay Brown, son of Barry and Caroline Brown of Wynewood, Pennsylvania…

Bride and Groom

Ms. Nancy Rodgers, an independent graphic designer, is to be married to Mr. Christopher Bollman, an associate with Whiteman, Jones & Kotter. Ms. Rodgers is a daughter of the late Patsy and Abraham Rodgers of Saddle Brook, New Jersey. Mr. Bollman is the son of Gregory and Emily Bollman of Phoenix, Arizona. A spring wedding is planned.

When sending in your announcement to your local paper, be sure to include your and your fiancé's daytime phone numbers just in case there are any questions regarding your submission. You don't want to give the newspaper any reason not to run the announcement.

OTHER PEOPLE'S PARTIES

While you're busy planning your wedding, your loved ones will be busy planning events in your honor, starting with the engagement party. The first engagement bash is hosted by the bride's parents, although others in your life—the groom's parents, coworkers, friends—are free to throw additional engagement parties. Next, the maid-of-honor and bridesmaids plan both the bridal shower and the bachelorette party. On the groom's side, the best man and groomsmen mastermind a bachelor party.

For the bride and groom, these fêtes are an opportunity to sit back, relax, coo over lovely gifts and enjoy basking in the warm glow of other people's best wishes. Savor the fact that, besides being consulted on date and time, you will have little control over invitations, food, venue or anything else. Show your gratitude to the hosts or hostesses with a brief toast during the event and thank-you notes sent soon afterward.

Chapter Three

INVITATIONS

The save-the-date card and the invitation are the first wedding-associated "pieces," in marketing parlance, that your guests will receive. Functionally, they communicate logistics. Stylistically, through choice of paper, font and formality (or informality) of language, they telegraph tone and theme: Is it a formal or informal wedding? Classic traditional or modern with a touch of whimsy? Since these pieces are brief, each detail is a clue that's up for interpretation. Think about what kind of impression you want to make.

Save-the-Date Cards

ONCE CUSTOMARY ONLY FOR COUPLES who were marrying over a holiday weekend, expecting a large number of out-of-town guests or planning a destination wedding, the save-the-date is now *de rigueur* for most. People are busy. They need more notice than the six-to-eight weeks the invitation provides. Notify them as soon as you know the wedding date and locale so they can ink—or upload—your wedding into their datebooks, arrange transportation and lodging and plan around the event as the month approaches.

This is especially necessary if you're marrying in the popular months of June through October and if you're at a stage in life (late twenties, early thirties) when your peers' main weekend activity six months out of the year is attending weddings. Mail your save-the-date cards six months in advance, and your guests will have a built-in excuse—"What can we do? It's postmarked a week before yours!"—when they're pinned to the wall by a "competing" bride and groom.

> *THE MOMENT MY EYES FELL ON HIM,*
> *I WAS CONTENT.*
> —EDITH WHARTON

WHAT SHOULD THEY SAY?

A save-the-date announcement should include the following:

- *Who's getting married?* Names of the bride and groom should figure prominently!

- *When?* Date of wedding.

- *Will I need to travel?* List the wedding location and the name and contact info for a travel agent, if you've secured one to coordinate guests' travel and accommodations.

- *Will the invitation follow?* Yes, it may seem painfully obvious, but it's customary to include the words "Invitation to follow."

- *Optional:* the URL for your wedding website.

DESTINATION WEDDING SAVE-THE-DATES

A save-the-date for a destination wedding may necessarily resemble a booklet more than a card. Guests need more detailed information about transportation and lodging, especially if you're marrying in-season at a popular destination. Here are some of the pieces you should think about including in a destination wedding's save-the-date:

All of the standard information plus:

- *Itinerary.* A brief outline and description of what you've planned for each day. Only include events to which all guests are invited.

- *Lodging information.* A list of high, midrange and economy options with phone, e-mail and contact information for each.

- *Airline information.* Which airlines fly to your destination? What is an average fare?

- *Car rentals or transport* from the airport to the destination.

- *Special information.* Will your guests need a visa or inoculations?

- *What to wear?* What to expect in terms of weather and local style, as well as sports or physical activities.

> LOVE DOESN'T MAKE
> THE WORLD GO 'ROUND.
> LOVE IS WHAT MAKES
> THE RIDE WORTHWHILE.
> —FRANKLIN P. JONES

INVITATIONS

THE WEDDING INVITATION is truly in a category of its own. What other piece of mail carries so many layers of promise: of tradition upheld, of love everlasting, of elegance personified? Yes, you've told your family and friends. You've sent them save-the-dates. Still, it's not real until they're holding an invitation in their hands—until it's there in black and white.

What you must include: who's hosting, who's getting married, when the ceremony is scheduled to begin and where. Beyond that, the invitation wording is up to you. It's best to keep it simple to avoid any possible confusion. Also, you want to keep in mind the tone and degree of formality of the actual ceremony and reception.

> HERE'S TO ONE AND ONLY ONE,
> AND MAY THAT ONE BE HE
> WHO LOVES BUT ONE AND ONLY ONE,
> AND MAY THAT ONE BE ME.

Of course, wording becomes tricky when family situations are unconventional. The first names mentioned on the invitation are traditionally the people who are footing the bill. If those people include the bride's stepfather and the groom's widowed mother, the wording is not so clear-cut.

Some general guidelines:

- Each adult member of a family receives his or her own invitation.

- Never use the phrase "and family." All the children's names should be spelled out.

- Names are written in full: no nicknames, initials or abbreviations, except for Mr., Mrs. and Ms. Write out titles for doctors, clergy, judges and military rank.

- Times are written out:

  "at half past two o'clock in the afternoon"

  or

  "at six o'clock in the evening"

  instead of

  "at 2:30 p.m."

  and

  "at 6 p.m."

TELLING PEOPLE
WHERE YOU'RE REGISTERED

Though it may seem the height of common sense, the words "the couple is registered at" should never appear on any piece of wedding stationery. Printing this information is considered to be in poor taste. The reasoning goes that guests will know to approach you, your parents or your attendants to ask where you've registered. Today, some wedding websites allow guests to search multiple stores' registries at once. If you're concerned that your guests won't think of asking and will assume you have no registry, you can encourage your parents and attendants to gently spread the word.

- Dates are written out: "on Saturday, the sixteenth of June, two thousand and seven"

Here are some suggested wordings to help you around a variety of situations:

- Bride's parents are hosting (traditional): (If groom's parents are hosting, switch order of names.)

MR. AND MRS. JOHN SMITH

REQUEST THE HONOR OF YOUR PRESENCE

AT THE MARRIAGE OF THEIR DAUGHTER

KATHERINE ELIZABETH

TO

JONATHAN PETER JONES

SATURDAY, THE TWENTIETH OF OCTOBER

TWO THOUSAND AND SEVEN

AT FIVE O'CLOCK IN THE EVENING

ST. PETER BASILICA CATHEDRAL

15 ST. PETER DRIVE

PALERMO, ILLINOIS

- Bride's parents are hosting (familiar):
  (*Note:* Mentioning the groom's parents, even if they're not sharing in the cost, is a thoughtful thing to do. Wedding planners urge couples to be inclusive—this is no time to be divisive.)

DOCTORS FREDERICK AND RUTH BUCK

REQUEST THE PLEASURE OF YOUR COMPANY

AT THE MARRIAGE OF THEIR DAUGHTER

HANNAH ALISON

TO

KARL EVAN KANTOR

LIEUTENANT, UNITED STATES ARMY,

SON OF

ROBERT AND PATRICIA KANTOR

FRIDAY, THE THIRTY-FIRST OF DECEMBER

TWO THOUSAND AND SEVEN

AT FIVE O'CLOCK IN THE EVENING

BETH EL SYNAGOGUE

5224 WEST TWENTY-SIXTH STREET

ST. LOUIS PARK, MINNESOTA

- Bride's parents are hosting (modern):

THOMAS AND DOROTHY ALDEN

JOYOUSLY INVITE YOU

TO THE WEDDING CELEBRATION OF

JODY NAOMI ALDEN

AND

GAVIN HEYWARD ROCKFORD

SATURDAY, THE THIRD OF SEPTEMBER

TWO THOUSAND AND SEVEN

AT FIVE O'CLOCK IN THE EVENING

SANDY LANE BEACH

SANDY LANE HOTEL

ST. JAMES, BARBADOS

• Bride's divorced parents are hosting:

DOCTOR RUSS ZATZ

AND

THE HONOURABLE SANDRA CARTWRIGHT

REQUEST THE PLEASURE OF YOUR COMPANY

AT THE MARRIAGE OF THEIR DAUGHTER

BEATRICE PLANTER ZATZ

TO

GEOFFREY ERIC PRENDERGAST

SATURDAY, THE SIXTEENTH OF OCTOBER

TWO THOUSAND AND SEVEN

AT FIVE O'CLOCK IN THE EVENING

FIRST UNITARIAN UNIVERSALIST CHURCH

1187 FRANKLIN STREET

SAN FRANCISCO, CALIFORNIA

- Bride's widowed mother is hosting with her husband, the bride's stepfather:

GENERAL AND MRS. MAKAYLIA ROBINSON

REQUEST THE PLEASURE OF YOUR COMPANY

AT THE MARRIAGE OF MRS. ROBINSON'S DAUGHTER

CHRISTINA LISBETH HINGSTON

TO

ELIAS JONAH HARVEY

MONDAY, THE THIRTY-FIRST OF MAY

TWO THOUSAND AND SEVEN

AT FIVE O'CLOCK IN THE EVENING

THE TERRACE

THE FOUR SEASONS HOTEL

ONE LOGAN SQUARE

PHILADELPHIA, PENNSYLVANIA

- Bride and groom are hosting:

MS. MARGARET TANYA FLINT

AND

MR. DAVID EDWARD CONNAUGHT

REQUEST THE HONOR OF YOUR PRESENCE

AT THEIR MARRIAGE

SATURDAY, THE FIFTH OF MAY

TWO THOUSAND AND SEVEN

AT FIVE O'CLOCK IN THE EVENING

KERN TERRACE AND SCULPTURE GARDEN

MUSEUM OF CONTEMPORARY ART

220 EAST CHICAGO AVENUE

CHICAGO, ILLINOIS

DRESS CODE

If you desire to look out upon a sea of dashing men and glamorous dames, you can't afford to be subtle about this wish. In these uncertain times, even an engraved invitation on the heaviest stock—Hello, people! Dress up!—may fall on deaf ears. There's no guarantee that your guests will arrive in black tie unless it's very clearly stated on the invitation. A suitable location is the bottom right-hand corner. What's the code for mandating different degrees of formal dress?

Black Tie: Evening dresses (short or long) for women; tuxedos for men.

Black Tie, Long Gown: Not common but found occasionally.

Black Tie Optional: Evening dresses (short or long) for women; tuxedos or dark suits for men.

Creative Tie: A dress other than black for women; a tuxedo or suit with a colorful twist (i.e. patterned cummerbund) for men.

No Children, Please

Should you decide on an adults-only affair, you'll need to be explicit about informing those with little ones. Spread the word even before you send out invitations: tell your

> *THE BEST AND MOST BEAUTIFUL*
> *THINGS IN THE WORLD*
> *CANNOT BE SEEN OR EVEN TOUCHED.*
> *THEY MUST BE FELT WITH THE HEART.*
> —HELEN KELLER

wedding party and relatives and ask them to initiate some targeted word of mouth.

Reinforce the message by addressing the envelope only to the adults. If you're still worried that someone won't get the message (and people do tend to assume that their own kids are the exception), opt for a detailed reply card that includes names of the invitees.

ADDITIONAL INVITATION PIECES

RECEPTION CARD If the ceremony and reception are in the same place, you can add "dinner and dancing to follow" right on the invitation, below the essential details about the ceremony. If the two events are in different places, include a separate card with reception information. It's possible that you want to invite a small group to the ceremony and a larger group to the party, or vice versa, in which case, the latter will receive only the appropriate invite.

Your reception card should include the following information:

What is it? The reception.

When? Time of day.

Where? Location.

Suggested wording for the reception enclosure card:

RECEPTION

AT SIX O'CLOCK IN THE EVENING

ST. REGIS HOTEL

3660 NORTH LAKE SHORE DRIVE

CHICAGO, ILLINOIS

REPLY CARD   Vintage etiquette dictates that no card be inserted and that guests take it upon themselves to send a formal letter of acceptance or regret using his or her personal stationery. This is not a reliable option, as few guests know this rule anymore and you may end up with one or two letters and no idea of actual attendance. Instead, go with the traditional option: a card with a brief message in the lower left-hand corner that reads: "The favor of a reply is requested before the first of June," or "Kindly respond by June 1." Respondents can use the blank space to write a personal message. Fold the funniest or most poignant into your wedding scrapbook. Or choose a more user-friendly route: the fill-in-the-blank reply card is best for busy guests with little time to spare on crafting personal messages. The format:

THE FAVOR OF A REPLY IS REQUESTED

BEFORE THE FIRST OF JUNE.

M_____

__ ACCEPTS WITH PLEASURE.

__ DECLINES WITH REGRETS.

or

THE FAVOR OF A REPLY IS REQUESTED

BEFORE THE FIRST OF JUNE.

M_____

WILL _____ ATTEND.

Or if you need people to reply for more than one event—a rehearsal dinner, a bridal luncheon, a postwedding brunch, etc.—list each event to be checked off or not.

Be sure to include a stamped reply-card envelope addressed to whomever is in charge of the guest list.

Note: Some of your guests may forget to write in their names, or they may have illegible handwriting. Solve this problem by numbering your guest list, then inconspicuously writing the corresponding number on the back of each response card.

MAP/HOTEL INFORMATION CARD *Map information:* Sometimes the venue has a map you can reprint on your cards. Or you may decide that a hand-drawn map would be clearer. Make sure all road names and major landmarks are easy to read. The map should include the hotels where you've reserved blocks of rooms, the ceremony locale and the reception venue. Also include clear and explicit directions to the ceremony and reception venues from several starting points.

Hotel information: List the names and phone numbers of two or three hotels where you've reserved rooms.

ALL TOGETHER NOW

The invitation and insertions sit inside an inner envelope that is addressed in a more informal manner to all the invitees at the address, including children. The outer envelope is addressed in a formal manner only to the primary guest or guests. The tradition of two envelopes dates to the mid-eighteenth century, when well-to-do hosts sent invitations by messengers on horseback. Messengers handed the sealed envelope to the servant at the door of each guest's home, then the butler discarded the soiled outer envelope and placed the clean inner envelope on a silver tray for presentation. Here are some examples of varying formality of language:

For a married couple:
Outer envelope: Mr. and Mrs. Peter Hutchinson
Inner envelope: Mr. and Mrs. Hutchinson

For a married couple where the wife kept her maiden name:
Outer envelope: Mrs. Bette Latham and
    Mr. Todd Hughes
Inner envelope: Mrs. Latham and Mr. Hughes

For an unmarried couple who live together (always list the names in alphabetical order):

Outer envelope: Mr. Timothy Lee and
    Ms. Robin Morgan
Inner envelope: Mr. Lee and Ms. Morgan

For a single woman:
Outer envelope: Ms. Katie Dexter
Inner envelope: Ms. Dexter and Guest

For a family (listing names of children under eighteen on the outer envelope is optional; if they're invited, they should be listed on the inner envelope):
Outer envelope: Mr. and Mrs. Arthur Post
    and Philip Post

Inner Envelope: Mr. and Mrs. Post and Philip,
Molly and Jane

ORDER Lay out all of your invitation pieces in piles on a clean, uncluttered table in the following order. Assemble them (from bottom to top) inside the unsealed inner envelope:

Invitation

Tissue paper

Reception card

Map/hotel info cards

Response envelope

Response card (tucked under flap of response envelope)

Now, slip the inner envelope inside the outer envelope with the guest's name facing the back. Address the outer envelope. Affix a pretty stamp and cart the boxes to the nearest post office.

> WHERE THERE IS LOVE, THERE IS LIFE.
> —MAHATMA GANDHI

Chapter Four

MORE PREWEDDING WORDS

A great way to keep in touch with all of your wedding guests during the months before the ceremony is to create a wedding website with continuous updates on events and logistics and extras like blogging about wedding planning or a page that recounts your love story. There are a few other details to consider, too, before you dive into the ceremony.

Going Online

Wedding Websites:
If You Build It, They Will Come

Like everything else having to do with your wedding, your website—should you choose to build one—should reflect your own personalities. The potential is infinite.

- Would you like the site to act as a storehouse for logistical information having to do with the wedding weekend, including travel and lodging information and the schedule of events?

- Would you like the site to provide details about you and your spouse: how you met, what you love about each other, why you're looking forward to the wedding?

A site can lie anywhere on the continuum between purely logistical to highly personalized. If you and your spouse are private people, stick with the former. If you choose to go the personal route, don't include anything that you wouldn't want a future employer to turn up during a Google search.

Once you've launched the site, send a group e-mail with a link to let guests know where to find it.

> *'TWAS NOT INTO MY EAR YOU WHISPERED,*
> *BUT INTO MY HEART.*
> —*JUDY GARLAND*

Here are some features to consider:

LOGISTICAL INFORMATION

- *Where to stay:* Names of hotels, their amenities and contact information.

- *How to get there:* Transportation information to your wedding, including airlines and information on rental cars. Also, driving times from the most common destinations.

- *What to do:* Top tourist sites in the area.

- *Where to eat:* A few options in all price ranges for breakfast, dinner and lunch.

- *Maps and driving directions* to each event.

One thing to remember: do not think of the website as a substitute for an invitation insert. Providing this information is necessary for those on your guest list.

PERSONAL INFORMATION

- *Your story:* The short tale of how you and your betrothed met, courted and decided to marry. (One creative way to do this is to tell your story through your e-mails. If you've saved your correspondence from the beginning, go through and pick a few from each phase of the relationship and arrange them in order, possibly illustrated by photos.)

- *The wedding party:* Introductions to each, possibly including photos and write-ups that explain how you know each person. Write it yourself or ask each of your attendants to come up with something.

- *Photo gallery:* Photos of you and your partner, the wedding party, the ceremony and reception sites.

- *Links to online registries:* If you've decided to set up a "Honeymoon Registry," where guests can pay for different parts of your honeymoon, this is easiest to set up online.

> *HERE'S TO THE MAN WHO WON*
> *NOT JUST MY HEART,*
> *BUT ALSO MY MOTHER'S APPROVAL.*

CYBERCOMMUNICATION

E-mail makes itself useful even in the über-traditional realm of wedding planning. It's not surprising, as there are so many details to address during the months leading up to the celebration, and typing up a quick missive is a great time-saver. Plus, it creates a handy "paper trail" that allows you to consult past exchanges in a jiffy if you're organized about saving all the e-mails in a "wedding" folder in your mail application. (The very organized will also have subfolders: florist, photographer, mother-in-law, etc.)

Hitting "send" is so easy, it's tempting to use e-mail for everything, but there are certain communiqués that shouldn't enter the cyber-realm. Here's a quick guide:

- Appropriate uses of e-mail
  - For sending e-mails to the maid of honor and bridesmaids as a group about logistics: dress fittings, delegating duties, bachelorette-weekend details, etc.

- For informal invitations to attendants: to dress shopping, to gatherings to address the invitations, to non–wedding-related get-togethers when planning is driving you up a wall.

- For sending around pictures of dresses that are currently in contention.

- For making arrangements with vendors.

- For announcing your engagement to friends.

• Inappropriate uses of e-mail

- To ask someone to be your attendant.

- To invite someone to your wedding.

- To send anything you wouldn't want to end up in the wrong in-box (i.e., venting about momzilla-in-law).

- To thank anyone who's been an integral part of the wedding-planning process, for example, attendants, parents and anyone who has hosted a prewedding party. Traditionally brides gift their bridesmaids during a bridesmaids' luncheon, and groomsmen and other notables receive gifts during the rehearsal dinner. And, of course, all gifts should be accompanied by heartfelt, handwritten thank-you notes.

WELCOME PACK

HOTELS ARE USUALLY HAPPY to place welcome bags, baskets or programs in your guests' rooms before their arrival. Even if you've sent a welcome letter listing events and activities for the wedding weekend, preparing a program of the weekend's whats, wheres and whens serves as an easy reminder. This is also an opportunity to include supplemental information, including

> *NEVER ABOVE YOU.*
> *NEVER BELOW YOU.*
> *ALWAYS BESIDE YOU.*
> —WALTER WINCHELL

maps, tourism brochures, maybe even that month's issue of the city magazine or a copy of a guidebook to the area. If you have the time and inclination, gift out-of-town guests with essential supplies: a bottle of water with custom "Jeff and Jennifer" labels, area delicacies, flip-flops in boy and girl colors. (This is a perfect project for a mother of the bride or mother of the groom.)

CANCELLATION CARDS

HAVING TO ANNOUNCE A POSTPONED or canceled wedding is unfortunate but not as unfortunate as guests getting all dressed up and showing up to an empty church. You must inform your guests as soon as possible. The best way is to send out printed cards. Specific reasons for the cancellation or postponement need not be included. The only time a reason is given is when the change is due to an illness or death in the family.

The card's wording is similar to an invitation:

> MR. AND MRS. PETER FLETCHER
>
> ANNOUNCE THAT THE MARRIAGE OF
>
> THEIR DAUGHTER,
>
> MAY JUSTINE FLETCHER
>
> TO
>
> ANTHONY VITOLY
>
> WILL NOT TAKE PLACE/HAS BEEN POSTPONED

Or, if the cause is an illness or death in the family:

> MR. PETER FLETCHER
>
> REGRETS THAT THE DEATH OF HIS WIFE
>
> OBLIGES HIM TO RECALL THE INVITATIONS
>
> TO THE WEDDING OF HIS DAUGHTER
>
> MAY JUSTINE FLETCHER
>
> TO
>
> ANTHONY VITOLY

Chapter Five

THE CEREMONY

There's so much prewedding work to do that it's easy to make the mistake of leaving the ceremony until the last minute. This would be a shame, because the ceremony is the centerpiece of the celebration. The words spoken by your officiant and by you and your fiancé and by whomever you choose to read are the words that send you into the world as a married couple. They should be well chosen, with your own tastes and personalities in mind.

ORDER OF THE CEREMONY

THE BASIC ORDER of the wedding ceremony—the part sandwiched between the processional and recessional—in most circumstances is as follows:

Processional

Opening remarks

Charge to the couple ("Do you, Tracy, take Todd, etc., etc....")

Vows

Readings and unity rituals

Ring exchange

Closing remarks

Pronouncement of marriage

Recessional

TO US, WE MAY NOT HAVE
IT ALL TOGETHER,
BUT TOGETHER WE HAVE IT ALL!

Types of Ceremonies

NO MATTER IF THEY'RE CIVIL or religious, most ceremonies have the same major components. The amount of leeway you have in choosing the words that make up these components depends on which type of ceremony you choose. At one end of the spectrum is the Roman Catholic ceremony, where customization is limited to helping choose the readings, prayers and psalms from the scriptures. At the other end is a civil ceremony, where anything goes.

Whatever type you choose, ask the officiant up front what they include in their "standard" ceremony. Some will hand you an actual transcript. Your second question should be: "What's required and what's up for negotiation?" Again, it's case by case. Here's what to expect from some of the more common options:

Civil Ceremonies

You have the freedom to incorporate any vow, unity ritual, reading or song. Couples often pull unity rituals from a variety of cultures and mix them together. Here are a few of the more common options:

Handfasting (Celtic): The couple's hands are tied together with string in a "love knot" after the vows and ring exchange as the officiant explains

> *WHATEVER SOULS ARE MADE OF,*
> *HIS AND MINE ARE THE SAME.*
> —*EMILY BRONTË*

that the bride and groom are bound together by the vows that they have made.

Circling (Jewish): Traditionally, the bride circles the groom seven times once they reach the *chuppah* (canopy under which the bride and groom stand during the ceremony). The circling represents the seven wedding blessings and also that the groom is at the center of her world. Many couples modernize the ritual by circling each other.

Unity candle (Catholic): The officiant explains the unity candle's meaning as the bride and groom light the same candle with two separate candles. This symbolizes their two lives joined together.

Jumping the broom (African-American): Together the couple sweeps in a circle, then they place the broom on the ground, join hands and jump. They are sweeping away evil spirits and jumping together into a new home and a new life.

With a civil ceremony, you also have leeway in your choice of officiant: a civil ceremony can be conducted by a judge, town clerk, mayor, notary public or other non-religious legal official. In some states—Alaska, California and Massachusetts—anyone is allowed to register as a justice of the peace for the day. In others—Florida, Maine and South Carolina—those who meet residency requirements can be notarized and qualify to conduct marriage ceremonies.

RELIGIOUS CEREMONIES

Each religion has its own wedding traditions, rules and customs. Often, the precise requirements depend on the branch and affiliation. Here are some basics regarding some major U.S. religions. Don't be afraid to ask your officiant if you can change some aspects of the standard service to better reflect your own beliefs. Again, the response will differ depending on orthodoxy and congregation.

PROTESTANT This is the most well-represented American wedding, the same one you see over and over again in the movies where the minister calls the ceremony to worship with the words, "Dearly beloved, we are gathered here today in the presence of God....," which come from the *Episcopalian Book of Common Prayer.* As you've seen on screen, Protestant ceremonies also include the giving-away of the bride, the blessing and prayers. There's no set liturgy, so there are opportunities to infuse the ceremony with some personal touches. How much depends on the specific denomination and congregation.

ROMAN CATHOLIC The ceremony usually includes a full mass (called a nuptial mass), including communion. In Roman Catholicism, marriage is one of the seven sacraments, and it is a serious celebration. The format and content have been set in stone for many, many years, so all the couple needs to worry about is customizing the service through their choice of prayers, readings and hymns from scripture. The priest's homily or sermon refers to the marriage but focuses on God.

JEWISH While ceremonies can differ according to affiliation, synagogue and rabbi, there are some traditions that are common to all Jewish weddings. The bride and groom marry beneath a *chuppah;* they enact two wine rituals, drinking from a shared cup at the beginning and end of the ceremony; and the grand finale: the groom stomping on and breaking a wineglass. (This tradition symbolizes different things to different people: for some, the delicacy of the vessel represents the fragile nature of relationships; for others it's an allusion to the destruction of the Temple in Jerusalem.) At all Jewish weddings, the rabbi will read

> *WHAT GREATER THING IS THERE*
> *FOR TWO HUMAN SOULS THAN*
> *TO FEEL THAT THEY ARE JOINED...*
> *TO STRENGTHEN EACH OTHER...*
> *TO BE AT ONE WITH EACH OTHER*
> *IN SILENT UNSPEAKABLE MEMORIES.*
> —GEORGE ELIOT

passages from the *ketubah*, or marriage contract, as well as the seven marriage blessings.

To be considered valid, a Jewish wedding requires a *kinyan*, or a gift of value the groom gives to the bride. In ancient times, grooms gave their brides coins. This ritual has evolved into today's double ring exchange, a more equitable proposition since each gives something of value to the other. And most Jewish ceremonies lead into *yichud*, a short period (fifteen minutes or so) directly following the ceremony when the bride and groom retreat to a private room. (Long ago, the couple consummated the marriage, but now it's more common for the couple to breathe a sigh of relief and grab a quick bite to eat.)

MUSLIM The American-Muslim wedding can be offici-
ated by any Muslim person. The bride and groom must
each bring at least one witness. The ceremony follows the
style of the basic American civil ceremony, but it might be
in Arabic instead of English.

BUDDHIST In Buddhism, weddings are secular ventures,
not sacraments. There are no religious instructions dictat-
ing that people should wed. Accordingly, there is no such
thing as a typical Buddhist wedding. Historically, in Asian
Buddhist countries, marriages were arranged by a marriage broker. Once the match was made, an astrologer
divined an auspicious date and time of day for the wedding. This is sometimes done with American-Buddhist
weddings.

On the appointed day, the couple gathers at a
Buddhist temple or in any place as long as there is an altar
with flowers, candles, incense and a statue of Buddha. The
priest reads Buddha's words on marriage, and the couple
might take pinches of incense and place them on the altar
in front of the Buddha statue. There is a charge to the couple, a ring exchange and a pronouncement.

INTERFAITH Having more options always means that
more time and consideration go into making a decision,
and this is never truer than when it comes to planning an

> *LET US CELEBRATE THIS OCCASION*
> *WITH WINE AND SWEET WORDS.*
> —*LATIN PROVERB*

interfaith ceremony. Before diving in, it's important to secure an officiant or officiants to conduct the ceremony. (In some cities, rabbis and ministers have done the work for you, establishing "clergy teams" to accommodate increasingly common Jewish/Christian pairings.)

Once you've found an experienced religious officiant to advise you on what can and cannot be mixed together, you can begin to sift through the wedding traditions of both religions. Pick the words and rituals that appeal to you, and work with the officiant to pull everything together into a cohesive and meaningful whole.

VOWS

MOST FAITHS (and in many cases, denominations, congregations and officiants within those faiths) have their own versions of time-honored vows. The wordings listed here are standard, but keep in mind that your officiant might differ a bit.

Common Wordings

Here are a few variations of common wordings for a civil ceremony and for the same major religions discussed in the previous section. Some officiants pose the vows in the form of questions, to which you respond, "I will," or "I do." Others ask if you do, then they have you each repeat the vows in your own name.

Civil

[Name], I take you to be my lawfully wedded husband/wife. Before these witnesses I vow to love you and care for you as long as we both shall live. I take you with all your faults and your strengths as I offer myself to you with my faults and strengths. I will help you when you need help, and I will turn to you when I need help. I choose you as the person with whom I will spend my life.

[Groom],
You are my reason
to run, to dance, to see,
to think, to live, but most of all,
you are my reason to love.
To my husband, [Groom].
—Old Eskimo Indian Wedding Prayer

PROTESTANT

I, [state your name], take thee, [name], to be my lawful wife/husband, to have and to hold, from this day forward, for better, for worse, for richer, for poorer, in sickness and in health, to love and to cherish, till death do us part, according to God's holy ordinance; and thereto I pledge thee my faith as long as we both shall live.

I, [state your name], take thee, [name], to be my wife/husband, and these things I promise you: I will be faithful to you and be honest with you; I will respect, trust, help and care for you; I will share my life with you; I will forgive you as we have been forgiven and I will try with you better to understand ourselves, the world and God through the best and the worst of what is to come, as long as we live.

I, [state your name], take thee, [name], to be my wife/husband, and before God and these witnesses I promise to be a faithful and true husband/wife.

ROMAN CATHOLIC

I, [state your name], take thee, [name], to be my wife/husband. I promise to be true to you in good times and in bad, in sickness and in health. I will love and honor you all the days of my life.

JEWISH In a Jewish ceremony, vows are said as the rings are exchanged. The traditional ceremony involves only one ring: the bride's. The marriage is sealed when the groom places the ring on the bride's finger and says,

"Behold, you are consecrated to me with this ring according to the laws of Moses and Israel."

But many modern couples opt for double ring ceremonies so the bride can say something, too. She says,

"This ring is a symbol that thou art my husband in accordance with the laws of Moses and Israel."

In some conservative Jewish wedding ceremonies, the rabbi asks of the bride and groom:

"Do you, [name], take [name] to be your lawful wedded wife/husband to love, to honor, and to cherish?"

MUSLIM

Bride: *"I, [state your name], offer you myself in marriage in accordance with the instructions of the Holy Quar'an and the Holy Prophet, peace and blessing be upon Him. I pledge, in honesty and with sincerity, to be for you an obedient and faithful wife."*

Groom: *"I pledge, in honesty and sincerity, to be for you a faithful and helpful husband."*

> *My true-love hath my heart,*
> *and I have his,*
> *By just exchange,*
> *one for the other given:*
> *I hold his dear,*
> *and mine he cannot miss,*
> *There never was*
> *a better bargain driven.*
> —Sir Philip Sidney

Writing Your Own Vows

First, ask your officiant whether there are any words or terms from the established vows that you're required to use in order to render your marriage valid by the religion, as well as by the law. Write those down and then get to work writing the rest. Begin at least two months before your wedding date and plan to have a final draft ready at least two weeks to a month before the big day. The worst-case scenario would be rushing the writing of your vows while your mind is occupied with last-minute dress alterations or with choosing the perfect song for the mother-son dance to hand off to the bandleader.

> *BEING DEEPLY LOVED BY SOMEONE*
> *GIVES YOU STRENGTH;*
> *LOVING SOMEONE DEEPLY*
> *GIVES YOU COURAGE.*
>
> —*LAO-TZU*

Here are some tips for sailing through the process:

- *Look to the old standards* ("Do you promise to love, honor and cherish, etc., etc."). In these, you'll notice some recurring themes: love, faithfulness, honor, respect, caring, sharing, forgiveness and trust. According to generations of brides, grooms and their officiants, these are the qualities required for a successful marriage. Do you agree? Are these the most important tenets of marriage? What does marriage mean to you? Have this discussion with your intended and take notes.

- *Reminisce.* Schedule a date with your fiancé to think back and recall together the defining moments of your relationship. Recount your history to one another. Ask each other what's unusual and special about your relationship. Did you meet in an unusual way? When was the moment you "knew" it was forever? Some nebulous memories may be crystal-clear to your fiancé and vice versa. How does each of you bring out the best in the other? This exchange will remind both of you why you're committing so completely to each other.

- *Make use of any prewedding counseling* that is required by your officiant or place of worship. These sessions will bring up thoughts about marriage that you may not have considered. Incorporate them into your brainstorming sessions about your vows. What have you learned that you want to tell your partner about your future together?

- *Correspond.* Write a letter to your fiancé about why you are marrying him. Write a letter as if it's only for the eyes of your betrothed. This will rid you of the inhibitions that might creep in once you think about declaring your devotion in front of a roomful of people. This letter can evolve into actual vows, or it can simply be an exercise in overcoming writer's block.

- *Get inspired.* Go back to books that you remember as being especially moving. Dip into love poems and timeless romance narratives written by Shakespeare, Jane Austen or, for a more modern gal, Helen Fielding. How does your love story parallel your favorite fictional love story? What does that heroine or hero have in common with your real-life heroine or hero? Watch movies and keep a notebook or laptop nearby to take notes. Keep a binder or a box for pages ripped out of magazines, Internet printouts, photocopies of book pages and other raw source material to draw on later.

- *Consult one another.* Some couples share their vows with each other beforehand; some do not. If you choose the latter, at least make sure your vows are around the same length; you don't want one person to go on forever while the other person delivers three sentences.

And some guidelines for final preparations and delivery:

- *Edit.* Read your final draft aloud with an eye on the time. It should be no longer than a minute. (If you have to shave off some essential sentiments, use them in one of your toasts.)

> *HAPPY MARRIAGES BEGIN*
> *WHEN WE MARRY THE ONE WE LOVE,*
> *AND THEY BLOSSOM WHEN*
> *WE LOVE THE ONE WE MARRIED.*
> —SAM LEVENSON

- *Practice.* Say the vows aloud to yourself to be sure you're comfortable and there are no tongue twisters. Insert plenty of pauses for timed breathing. While you're reading aloud, imagine all your family members and friends standing nearby and edit accordingly if you have second thoughts about sharing any especially personal sentiments with a large crowd.

- *Put them on paper.* Most couples figure on being so nervous and filled with emotion that memorization is out of the question. Even if you're determined to memorize your vows, it's a good idea to have a backup. Write them on an index card the groom can store in the inside pocket of his suit or tuxedo jacket. The officiant, groom or maid of honor can hold on to the bride's.

> *THE MOMENT I HEARD MY FIRST*
> *LOVE STORY I BEGAN SEEKING YOU,*
> *NOT REALIZING THE SEARCH*
> *WAS USELESS.*
> *LOVERS DON'T MEET*
> *SOMEWHERE ALONG THE WAY.*
> *THEY'RE IN ONE ANOTHER'S SOULS*
> *FROM THE BEGINNING.*
> —*JALAL AL-DIN RUMI, PERSIAN LOVE POEM*

- *Anxious about public speaking?* As with standard religious vows, you can opt to write a mutual vow that you will both take, that the officiant will ask of you, and to which you'll respond, "I will" or "I do."

SAMPLES OF CUSTOMIZED VOWS

Notice that customized vows usually don't depart entirely from the old standards. The changes amount to cutting outdated language such as "honor and obey" in favor of language that stresses equality or to including specific values that weren't stressed in available scripted vows.

All of these couples maintain the sense of hallowedness

that's suitable for such a profound ceremony. Though it's possible to include something funny, the overall tone should be reverent. (You can go for laughs later, at the reception.) And while the sentiments are personal, none get too intimate. These vows are for each other, but they're also meant to be witnessed by an audience.

"Do you pledge to support each other's journey, to continually shine light on each other's virtue and support individual intuitions, even when doing so doesn't directly benefit you? Do you pledge to reinforce and complement each other's virtue?"

"I take you as my friend and love, beside me and apart from me, in laughter and in tears, in conflict and tranquillity, asking that you be none other than yourself, loving what I know of you, trusting what I do not know yet, in all the ways that life may find us."

"Do you, [name], offer yourself wholly and joyfully, and do you choose [name] as the person with whom you will share your life, in laughter and in tears, in conflict and tranquillity, loving what you know of her and trusting what you do not know yet?"

"I, [name], take you, [name], to be my wife. I promise above all else to live in truth with you and to communicate fully and fearlessly. I give you my hand and my

> *A HAPPY MARRIAGE IS*
> *A LONG CONVERSATION*
> *THAT ALWAYS SEEMS TOO SHORT.*
> *—ANDRÉ MAUROIS*

heart as a sanctuary of warmth and peace and pledge my love, devotion, faith and honor as I join my life to yours."

"[Name], you are my best friend and the one I want to share my life with. I will love you forever and stand by you always. I will be yours in times of plenty and in times of want. I will have faith in you and encourage you in everything you do. I will work with you to build a life together, and I will support you as you live your own independent life. I will be your friend, your lover and your partner for all the days of our lives."

"I, [name], take you, [name], to be none other than yourself, to share all the wonders of life by giving you space to learn and grow individually, by supporting and respecting your endeavors, by having faith in your love and by being trustworthy so that we may create a home of happiness and safety for all of our years and in all that life may bring."

"Today, I become your wife/husband. I promise to give and to receive, to speak and to listen, to inspire and to respond in all circumstances of our life together. I pledge you my love and my loyalty, my strength and my respect above all others—forever."

READINGS

LUCKY FOR US that so many others have managed to articulate their thoughts about love so beautifully. Long before Gutenberg invented the printing press, troubadours, poets, composers and scribes ate up weeks, years even, considering love's many attributes: passion, beauty, desire, unrequited and realized love, and its limits and boundlessness. Really, a ceremony could go on for hours, with a rotating cast of friends and family members reciting a litany of readings. The biggest challenge might be narrowing down the choices to the perfect two or three that express the character of your own relationship and your wishes for its future. If you find those perfect two or three, and then realize you have more readers than readings, one solution is to have multiple readers per reading:

have each read one or a few lines before passing it on to the next reader.

First, consult your officiant on what's allowed. Restrictions might apply in a religious ceremony, in which case your officiant can give you a list of approved pieces from which to choose. Otherwise, consider these ideas as you set out to find the perfect words:

WHAT TO CHOOSE?

- Who are your favorite poets or writers? Are there any that have special meaning to both of you as a couple? If not, are there any that either of you remember from high school or college literature classes as striking a chord?

- Are there any songs, movies or novels that have special meaning? Don't discount these options; songs are poetry set to music. Lyrics can be read aloud as if they were lines of poetry. Well-chosen, short passages from novels can be very poignant.

- Do any of the readings you're considering gel with the "theme" of your wedding, whether it's a medieval castle or a tropical beach?

- Don't limit yourself to words that hail from your own culture and religion. For example, you may have been raised Jewish and have chosen a

> *WHO WALKS A ROAD WITH LOVE*
> *WILL NEVER WALK THAT*
> *ROAD ALONE AGAIN.*
> —CHARLES THOMAS DAVIS

civil ceremony, but if there's a Buddhist meditation that rings true, by all means incorporate that into the ceremony's script.

- If a friend is a proficient singer and somewhat accomplished performer, you might consider asking him or her to sing during the ceremony.

- As far as length, readings should last from one to four or five minutes. Anything less is too short—when the reading is finished, the audience will have had just enough time to adjust to a new element being introduced into the ceremony. Anything longer will try anyone with a short attention span.

- Leave the content up to your reader(s). Ask him or her (them) to choose a reading, but make sure it has been cleared by the officiant first.

- If, after you choose your readings, you're left with a pile of extras that you love, you can always incorporate them in other ways: verbalized in toasts and speeches at the reception, printed in the program, written on the cake or printed on place cards or at the bottom or on the back of the menu cards.

WHO?

- There will be some close friends and family members whom you'd like to involve in the ceremony but who aren't in the wedding party. You can ask parents and grandparents even if they already have a special spot in the procession; having them read also is not overkill.

- Make sure the reader is comfortable with the reading material. Send it to the reader as far in advance as possible so that he or she can practice or let you know well ahead of time that he or she doesn't feel right saying the words you've asked to be read.

- When you send the text to the reader, make sure to include at the top the title and author, as well as its significance. Specifically ask the reader to recite this information before the reading.

- Allow enough time for readers to practice at the rehearsal—make sure everyone knows his or her cue, where to stand while reading and what will happen immediately afterward.

- Without sounding like your second-grade teacher, remind your readers of a few public-speaking basics: project, enunciate, breathe and speak slowly and with your head up (not bent down so the words disappear into the podium). Assure them there's plenty of time and no chance of being kicked out of the church if the ceremony goes a few minutes over.

When?

- If a venue is on the small side, a reader can simply stand in place when it's his or her turn to read.

If it's a large wedding, he or she should come up to the altar or podium and use the same microphone as the officiant.

- Consider selecting a few readings and interspersing them throughout the ceremony to parallel the development of your relationship: maybe the first is about friendship; the second, love; and the third, commitment and marriage.

- Your officiant will have advice on where to place the readings. They are usually spread out, with one right after the opening remarks, another after the vows and another after the ring exchange.

- Make sure all readers are invited to the rehearsal so that everyone is very familiar with their cues and, if they do need to approach an altar or podium, with where to sit in order to get there with ease.

TRADITIONAL RELIGIOUS READINGS

1 CORINTHIANS 13:4–8

Love is patient; love is kind. Love is not jealous, it does not put on airs, it is not snobbish. Love is never rude, it is not self-seeking, it is not prone to anger; neither does it brood over injuries. Love does not rejoice in what is wrong but

> # THERE IS ONLY ONE HAPPINESS IN LIFE,
> ## TO LOVE AND BE LOVED.
> —GEORGE SAND

rejoices with the truth. There is no limit to love's forbearance, to its trust, its hope, its power to endure.

Love never fails. Prophecies will cease, tongues will be silent, knowledge will pass away....There are in the end three things that last: faith, hope and love, and the greatest of these is love.

ECCLESIASTES 4:9–12

Two are better than one, because they have a good return for their toil. For if they fall, one will lift up his fellow; but woe to him who is alone when he falls and has not another to lift him up. Again, if two lie together, they are warm; but how can one be warm alone? And though a man might prevail against one who is alone, two will withstand him.

EPHESIANS 5:21–33

Submit yourselves one to another in the fear of God. Wives, show reverence for your own husbands, as unto the Lord. For the husband is the head of the wife, even *as Christ is the head of the church, and He is the savior of the body. Therefore as the church is subject unto Christ, so let the wives be to their own husbands in everything.*

Husbands, love your wives, even as Christ also loved the church, and gave Himself for it; that He might sanctify and cleanse it with the washing of water by the word; that He might present it to Himself a glorious church, not having spot, or wrinkle or any such thing; but that it should be holy and without blemish. So ought men to love their wives as their own body; He that loves his wife loves himself.

TWO SUCH AS YOU WITH
SUCH A MASTER SPEED
CANNOT BE PARTED NOR BE SWEPT AWAY
FROM ONE ANOTHER
ONCE YOU ARE AGREED
THAT LIFE IS ONLY LIFE FOREVERMORE
TOGETHER WING TO WING
AND OAR TO OAR
—ROBERT FROST

For no man ever yet hateth his own flesh; but nourishes and cherishes it, even as the Lord the church. For we are members of his body, of his flesh and of his bones. For this cause shall man leave his father and mother, and shall be joined unto his wife, and the two shall become one flesh. This mystery is a profound one and I am saying this as it refers to Christ and the church; however, let the husband love his wife as himself, and let the wife see that she respect her husband.

POETRY AND PROSE

Be sure to also read the short quotes throughout this book for inspiration.

Excerpt from *The Prophet* by Kahlil Gibran

Love has no other desire but to fulfill itself.
But if you love and must needs have desires, let
these be your desires:
To melt and be like a running brook that sings its
melody to the night.
To know the pain of too much tenderness.
To be wounded by your own understanding of love;
And to bleed willingly and joyfully.
To wake at dawn with a winged heart and give thanks
for another day of loving;

To rest at the noon hour and meditate love's ecstasy;
To return home at eventide with gratitude;
And then to sleep with a prayer for the beloved in
your heart and a song of praise on your lips.

Let Me Not to the Marriage of True Minds
by William Shakespeare

Let me not to the marriage of true minds
Admit impediments. Love is not love
Which alters when it alteration finds,
Or bends with the remover to remove:
O, no! it is an ever-fixed mark
That looks on tempests and is never shaken;
It is the star to every wand'ring bark,
Whose worth's unknown, although his heighth be taken.
Love's not Time's fool, though rosy lips and cheeks
Within his bending sickle's compass come;
Love alters not with his brief hours and weeks,
But bears it out even to the edge of doom.
If this be error and upon me proved,
I never writ, nor no man ever loved.

If Thou Must Love Me by Elizabeth Barrett Browning

If thou must love me, let it be for naught
Except for love's sake only. Do not say,
'I love her for her smile—her look—her way
Of speaking gently, for a trick of thought
That falls in well with mine, and certes brought
A sense of pleasant ease on such a day'—
For these things in themselves, Beloved, may
Be changed, or change for thee—and love, so wrought,
May be unwrought so. Neither love me for
Thine own dear pity's wiping my cheeks dry:
A creature might forget to weep, who bore
Thy comfort long, and lose thy love thereby!
But love me for love's sake, that evermore
Thou mayst love on, through love's eternity.

The First Day by Christina Rossetti

I wish I could remember the first day,
First hour, first moment of your meeting me;
If bright or dim the season it might be;
Summer or winter for aught I can say.
So unrecorded did it slip away,
So blind was I to see and to forsee,
So dull to mark the budding of my tree
That would not blossom yet for many a May.

If only I could recollect it! Such
A day of days! I let it come and go
As traceless as a thaw of bygone snow.
It seemed to mean so little, meant so much!
If only now I could recall that touch,
First touch of hand in hand!—Did one but know!

She Walks In Beauty by Lord Byron

She walks in beauty, like the night
Of cloudless climes and starry skies;
And all that's best of dark and bright
Meets in her aspect and her eyes,
Thus mellow'd to that tender light
Which Heaven to gaudy day denies.

One shade the more, one ray the less,
Had half impair'd the nameless grace
Which waves in every raven tress,
Or softly lightens o'er her face;
Where thoughts serenely sweet express
How pure, how dear their dwelling-place.

And on that cheek, and o'er that brow,
So soft, so calm, yet eloquent,
The smiles that win, the tints that glow,
But tell of days in goodness spent—

> ## *I WOULD BE FRIENDS WITH YOU*
> ## *AND HAVE YOUR LOVE.*

A mind at peace with all below,
A heart whose love is innocent.

To My Dear and Loving Husband by Anne Bradstreet

If ever two were one, then surely we.
If ever man were loved by wife, then thee.
If ever wife was happy in a man,
Compare with me, ye women, if you can.
I prize thy love more than whole Mines of gold,
Or all the riches that the East doth hold.
My love is such that Rivers cannot quench,
Nor ought but love from thee, give recompence.
Thy love is such I can no way repay.
The heavens reward thee manifold, I pray.
Then while we live, in love let's so persever,
That when we live no more, we may live ever.

Excerpt from *Love* by Samuel Taylor Coleridge

ALL thoughts, all passions, all delights,
Whatever stirs this mortal frame,
All are but ministers of Love,
    And feed his sacred flame.

Oft in my waking dreams do I
Live o'er again that happy hour,
When midway on the mount I lay,
    Beside the ruin'd tower.

The moonshine, stealing o'er the scene,
Had blended with the lights of eve;
And she was there, my hope, my joy,
    My own dear Genevieve!

She lean'd against the armèd man,
The statue of the armèd Knight;
She stood and listen'd to my lay,
    Amid the lingering light.

Few sorrows hath she of her own,
My hope! my joy! my Genevieve!
She loves me best whene'er I sing
    The songs that make her grieve.

I play'd a soft and doleful air;
I sang an old and moving story—
An old rude song, that suited well
    That ruin wild and hoary.

She listen'd with a flitting blush,
With downcast eyes and modest grace;
For well she knew I could not choose
    But gaze upon her face.

That sometimes from the savage den,
And sometimes from the darksome shade,
And sometimes starting up at once
    In green and sunny glade—

There came and look'd him in the face
An angel beautiful and bright;
And that he knew it was a Fiend,
    This miserable Knight!

O *Mistress Mine* by William Shakespeare

O mistress mine, where are you roaming?
O stay and hear! your true-love's coming
    That can sing both high and low;
Trip no further, pretty sweeting,
Journeys end in lovers' meeting—
    Every wise man's son doth know.

What is love? 'tis not hereafter;
Present mirth hath present laughter;
    What's to come is still unsure:
In delay there lies no plenty,—
Then come kiss me, Sweet-and-twenty,
    Youth's a stuff will not endure.

> MAY WE EACH BE SHELTER
> TO THE OTHER;
> MAY WE EACH BE WARMTH
> TO THE OTHER;
> AND MAY OUR DAYS BE GOOD
> AND LONG UPON THIS EARTH.
> —INSPIRED BY AN APACHE INDIAN PRAYER

Marriage Morning by Alfred Tennyson

Light, so low upon earth,
You send a flash to the sun.
Here is the golden close of love,
All my wooing is done.
Oh, the woods and the meadows,
Woods where we hid from the wet,
Stiles where we stay'd to be kind,
Meadows in which we met!

Light, so low in the vale
You flash and lighten afar,
For this is the golden morning of love,
And you are his morning start.
Flash, I am coming, I come,
By meadow and stile and wood,
Oh, lighten into my eyes and heart,
Into my heart and my blood!

Heart, are you great enough
For a love that never tires?
O heart, are you great enough for love?
I have heard of thorns and briers,
Over the meadow and stiles,
Over the world to the end of it
Flash for a million miles.

From *Jane Eyre* by Charlotte Brontë

> I have for the first time found what I can truly love—I have found you. You are my sympathy—my better self—my good angel—I am bound to you with a strong attachment. I think you good, gifted, lovely; a fervent, a solemn passion is conceived in my heart; it leans to you, draws to you my centre and spring of life, wraps my existence about you—and, kindling in pure, powerful flame, fuses you and me in one.

EXCHANGING RINGS

THE NEXT BIT OF CEREMONY to consider is the ring exchange. After exchanging vows, you will exchange wedding rings. As with the remarks made before the vows, the officiant may say a few words to explain the significance of the rings; if the ceremony is religious, the officiant might say a blessing over them. Then it's your turn.

Take your cue from your vows; this is where your words are translated into action as you make the gesture that seals the promise. If your vows are simple and traditional, go with a simple and traditional ring exchange: "With this ring, I thee wed." If you wrote vows, you may want to write a ring exchange to keep the tone and sentiments consistent.

> ### NOW JOIN YOUR HANDS,
> ### AND WITH YOUR HANDS YOUR HEARTS.
> —WILLIAM SHAKESPEARE

Another option is to fold the ring exchange into the vows and exchange rings when you say your "I wills," or "I dos." (In this case, the officiant will talk about the significance of the ring exchange before your begin your vows.)

EXCHANGES

PROTESTANT

In token and pledge of our constant faith and abiding love, with this ring, I thee wed, in the name of the Father and of the Son and of the Holy Spirit. Amen.

LUTHERAN

I give you this ring as a sign of my love and faithfulness. Receive this ring as a token of wedded love and faith.

BAPTIST

With this ring I thee wed and all my worldly goods I thee endow. In sickness and in health, in poverty or in wealth, till death do us part.

> *To say the words*
> *"love and compassion" is easy.*
> *But to accept that love*
> *and compassion are built*
> *upon patience and perseverance*
> *is not easy.*
> *Your marriage will be firm*
> *and lasting if you remember this.*
> *—Buddhist marriage homily*

CATHOLIC

Take this ring as a sign of my love and fidelity. In the name of the Father and of the Son and of the Holy Spirit.

In the name of the Father and of the Son and of the Holy Spirit. Take and wear this ring as a pledge of my fidelity.

JEWISH

Be sanctified to me with this ring, in accordance with the laws of Moses and Israel.

NONDENOMINATIONAL

I circle your finger with this ring of love and light as a constant reminder of my promises to you. May it be a symbol to you and to the world of my respect and love for you.

I give you this ring as a symbol of my enduring love. With it I wed you and give you my body, soul and heart.

Take and wear this ring as a symbol of our love. As this ring encircles your finger from this day forward, year in and year out, so will my love forever encircle you.

ENGRAVING IDEAS

Engraving your rings is a meaningful way to personalize a universal ritual (and it ensures that if your rings ever turn up in a lost and found, you'll know which ones are yours). Make sure you size the rings before you get them engraved, and ask to see samples of similar engravings on the same kind of material (gold is softer and thus easier to engrave than platinum) before you choose an engraver. As for content, remember that the two rings can—and often do—have different engravings. And since there's not much room, you'll need to come up with a succinct way to say "I love you, forever" in approximately eight words.

Some ideas:

- "Love you, forever" or simply "Forever" with your initials and/or wedding date.

- On the groom's ring, have the initials of the bride, along with the word *to*, and then the initials of the groom. On the bride's ring, have the initials of the groom, along with the word *to*, and then the initials of the bride. Example: For Donna Evelyn Martin and Brian Andrew Green, his ring would be engraved as: DEM to BAG; her ring would be engraved as: BAG to DEM.

- Your first names (or initials) and wedding date. Example: Donna and Brian, 8/22/06.

- *Amor vincit omnia* ("Love conquers all" in Latin).

- "All you need is love" (a meaningful song lyric).

- Your astrological symbols (or some other meaningful symbol).

- A snippet from your vows.

- Your pet names for each other.

- *Te amo* ("I love you" in Italian).

- "Blessed be."

> *HERE'S TO THE HUSBAND—*
> *AND HERE'S TO THE WIFE;*
> *MAY THEY REMAIN LOVERS*
> *FOR THE REST OF THEIR LIFE.*

- *Vous et nul autre* ("You and no other" in French).

- *Ani L'dodi V'dodi Li* ("I am my beloved's, and my beloved is mine" in Hebrew, from the Song of Solomon 2:16).

CEREMONY PROGRAMS

HANDING OUT PROGRAMS at the ceremony makes your guests feel as if they're really participating. What should you include? Programs can range from single sheets to bound booklets.

Here are the basics:

- Who's who: the names of everyone in your wedding party and their relationship to you, especially if they have a different last name.

- Officiant's name.

- Anyone else in attendance who deserves an honorable mention.

- A detailed ceremony itinerary.

- Titles and authors of the readings along with the names of the readers and their relationship to you (i.e., "cousin of the bride" or "college roommate of the groom").

- Names of musical selections and their composers along with the names of the singers and their relationship to you, if there is one; if the singer is affiliated with the religious institution, i.e., if a cantor or a nun is singing the selection, do include his or her name.

- Explanation of special rituals, such as the reading of the *ketubah*, handfasting or jumping the broom.

- The requisite reminder to please turn off your cell phones, Blackberries and PDAs.

Extras:

- The readings in their entirety along with explanation of any special significance.

- A word about the venue, especially if it's a historic building or a place with special significance for the couple.

- Childhood or current photos of the bride and groom.

> GROW OLD WITH ME!
> THE BEST IS YET TO BE,
> THE LASTS OF LIFE,
> FOR WHICH THE FIRST WAS MADE.
> —ROBERT BROWNING

- Consider matching the invitation motif.

- Special tributes to deceased friends or relatives.

- The words of the prayers and songs included in the ceremony.

- Your vows.

- Quotes and poems that may not be in the ceremony but that you wished you'd had room for (maybe printed on the back or around the edges, so people know they're not part of the actual ceremony).

- A brief story of how you met, a funny courtship or proposal story.

Chapter Six

THE RECEPTION

Congratulations! Now's the time to let loose and celebrate. You are officially married. The time to be tearful and reverent has passed, and now it's time to mark that shift in words. Toasts are light-hearted and possibly bawdy (though nothing should offend, consider the youngest and oldest guests who will be present), favors are stylish and fun and the musical selections tempt guests to take a turn or two on the dance floor.

TOASTS

THOUGH THE ORIGINS OF THE TOAST can not be unequivocally determined, it is believed that the term came from the old tradition of putting a piece of spiced toast into wine to improve the flavor. Since this wine and spiced toast combination was commonly used to offer good tidings, a metaphor arose that compared the honoree to the piece of toast— the honoree adds flavor to a situation just as the toast does to the wine. Though the tradition of adding toast to wine has passed, the use of the term remains strong.

A good toast should be short and easy to say, and it should be full of sentiment and wit. Not an easy combination.

WHO AND WHEN?

- Toasts usually begin after cocktails, once everyone has been seated for the meal and has been served a drink.

- Traditionally the best man serves as toastmaster. To get everyone's attention, he walks up to the

> *HERE'S TO MY MOTHER-IN-LAW'S DAUGHTER,*
> *HERE'S TO HER FATHER-IN-LAW'S SON;*
> *AND HERE'S TO THE VOWS WE'VE JUST TAKEN,*
> *AND THE LIFE WE'VE JUST BEGUN.*

microphone, introduces himself and begins. The maid of honor can serve as comaster, or she can simply make a toast after the best man. One or both should be given the responsibility of figuring out the toast order so they can keep the evening running smoothly and make sure no one feels slighted for not getting a turn at the mike.

• The groom responds to the best man and toasts his new wife and also offers thanks and appreciation to his parents, whether they are hosting the reception or not. In these modern times, it's becoming common for the bride to also make a toast to her new husband and her guests. Traditionally, though, the bride makes a toast at the rehearsal dinner, to her husband and to her in-laws, and the reception is the groom's domain.

- The toasts can continue, or they can be interspersed throughout the meal, between courses—a good option when there are a lot of toasts.

- Parents might want to toast, especially if they're hosting the reception, and so might other relatives and friends. The groom's parents typically toast at the rehearsal dinner, which can also be a good occasion for other family members and friends to say a few words. People might feel more comfortable sharing their sentiments in this more relaxed and casual setting, and this helps keep the number of toasts down during the wedding, freeing up time for eating, visiting and dancing.

- If there are still more people who'd like to toast but who didn't get a chance, there's always the postwedding brunch.

- If there is someone who would like to toast and who, for whatever reason, isn't part of the evening's agenda, the best man as toastmaster is responsible for letting this person know that it's not possible. The best man might say, "I'm sorry, but we've reached maximum capacity with the toasts. As it is, there's hardly time for the guests to enjoy their dinner."

- If you think someone might want to make a toast, you should ask and have him or her tell the maid of honor or best man before the reception so that person is factored into the schedule.

- At a Jewish wedding, the father of the bride begins the meal at the reception by saying a blessing over a loaf of challah bread. The blessing is sometimes preceded by a toastlike speech. At Christian and Catholic weddings, a blessing is said before the meal is served.

ETIQUETTE

- When you're being toasted, remain seated and don't raise your glass to yourself. Keep your focus on and listen closely to the person who's honoring you.

- If you're making a toast and you don't drink alcohol, ask the server for some other beverage.

- When you make a toast, stand up and walk to the microphone so that everyone can hear what you're saying. If going up to the microphone makes you extremely anxious, focus on whomever you're honoring while you're making the toast instead of looking around the room.

CONQUERING YOUR FEAR OF PUBLIC SPEAKING

- Practice, practice, practice. While you're practicing, notice where you pause naturally and indicate these pauses in your notes to remind yourself to breathe while you're at the mike.

- Find out beforehand exactly where your friends and family are sitting so that you can make eye contact with your support system as you deliver your toast. Their kind eyes will bolster your confidence.

- Remember that this is an easy crowd; they're at a wonderful party, and they're basking in the glow of enduring love. They want to love your toast. They want to laugh at your jokes.

- Though a few sips of wine may help, too much will definitely hurt. Don't drink in order to feel more relaxed for your toast. Alcohol is a depressant, and overdoing it may depress your ability to speak clearly, not to mention impairing your common sense.

WHAT TO SAY

Don't try to style yourself into a modern-day Shakespeare. Just talk as if you're talking to your friends (without any vulgarities or inappropriate anecdotes, of course). Keep it chatty, funny, poignant and short. Here are some ideas to get you started:

- Use someone else's words to start off the toast: Begin with a quote that begs further discussion, for example, "Someone once said, 'Everyone admits that love is wonderful and necessary, yet no one agrees on just what it is.' Well, I can't presume to provide you with a definition, but I do know that I feel it truly and deeply when I am with Lois…."

- This is a nice time to pay tribute to a deceased relative or friend whom you wish could have been there to witness this special day.

- Write the toast in advance and practice speaking it aloud, preferably to a live person, to get his or her feedback and to hone the structure and delivery to make the greatest impact.

> *WINTER TWILIGHT*
> *ON A WINDOW PANE*
> *I WRITE YOUR NAME.*
> —*JAPANESE HAIKU*

FOR THE RECEPTION

ESCORT CARDS AND PLACE CARDS

Escort cards are the small cards that tell guests where they're sitting at the reception. They're usually laid out alphabetically on a table outside the cocktail and reception room(s). They have each guest's name and table number. Once guests find their table, they can locate their seat by finding their place card, another small card with their name.

It's common to carry over the wedding's visual motif to the escort and place cards. You can also do so with the words. Consider naming the tables instead of giving them numbers. Name them for:

- Places you've traveled together as a couple.

- Landmarks, such as names of beaches or historic spots that are specific to the wedding venue or the couple's courtship.

- Titles of favorite books—maybe romantic ones— or names of favorite authors or poets.

- Names of paintings, artists or storied muses.

- Film titles or names of famous actors.

MENU CARDS

In order to print menu cards, you'll need to be sure of your menu and wine selections far enough in advance to order printed cards, unless you're having a small wedding, in which case the cards can be handwritten.

WHAT TO INCLUDE?

- A description of each course, along with wine selections.

- If you know you have guests with food allergies, notifications either that certain suspect dishes do or do not contain peanuts or shellfish or what- ever they may be allergic to.

- If the dishes have special significance, i.e., "What Lois ordered on Tom and Lois's first date," or "We used Great Aunt Elizabeth's famous maca- roon recipe."

- If there are special events that will take place or traditions that will be observed during the reception, you could also turn the menu cards into a "reception program."

FAVORS IDEAS

- Burn CDs and include liner notes that tell your story.

- The wedding readings from the ceremony, printed on parchment paper and tied in a scroll with a ribbon.

- Homemade regional preserves, cheese, hot sauce, cider, flowering bulbs—depending on your location and the season—with hand-printed labels, complete with the bride and groom's names, the wedding date and a heartfelt "thank you."

- Depending on your wedding's theme and tone, just about anything, from yo-yos to wine bottles, can be printed with your names and the wedding date.

- Printed cards that tell your guests where you've made a charity donation in their name.

- If the dinner is seated, one menu card to a place setting or two or three, framed, on a table.

- For a buffet, a card in front of each chafing and other dish on the buffet table.

GUEST BOOK

THE GUEST BOOK should be prominently placed just at the entrance to the reception or on a stand near the gift table in the reception room. A nice leather-bound blank book does the trick. Or spice it up a bit by giving your guests something to look at, such as photos of the bride and groom as kids and while they were dating. This is a great project for a creative wedding attendant or a close relative who doesn't live close by but who wants to be involved in some way.

Chapter Seven

AFTER THE WEDDING

Okay, you can put down your pen during the honeymoon, but once you're back, it's time to take care of a few more small tasks related to the wedding. First and foremost are thank-you notes for every gift you've received. Send them immediately upon your return or gift givers will wonder whether you've received the gift and, if you haven't, whether they should call the store to complain. You'll also run the risk of feeling awkward when you run into guests who are wondering why they haven't yet received a thank-you note.

Thank-you Notes

EACH GIFT GIVER RECEIVES ONE; it doesn't matter whether the person gave you a gift for your engagement, rehearsal dinner, bachelor party or bridal luncheon. It's best to keep on top of things and to send the notes out while the occasion is still fresh so you don't return from your honeymoon to a gargantuan task.

The basics of thank-you notes:

- *Keep track.* The best way to record gifts is to keep copies of all your invitation lists and in one column write notes next to the guest's name as soon as the gift arrives. Record any details that will come in handy when you're writing your thank-you note, such as the color and quantity, first impression, whether the gift card says anything particularly personal or clever and whether or not the card was signed. In the second column, indicate when a thank-you note goes out to that gift giver. Use a simple word-processing application to create a table on your computer.

- *Divide it up.* The bride and groom should share this task: he writes the notes to his family and friends, and she takes care of hers. If there are people who are friends of both, the bride and groom should both sign those notes.

- *Don't drag your feet.* If you can't send the note immediately, send it within at most one month after the gift was given. However, if you receive the gift before the wedding, do wait until after the wedding to send the thank-you note. Sending the thank-you note before the actual event has happened is admirable for its conscientiousness but can be a bit jarring for the gift giver.

- *Keep it simple.* Write five to six lines on stationery that matches or complements your wedding invitations. Personalize each note by mentioning specifics about the gift and why you like it and what you plan to use it for in the future. If the gift was money, specify what you plan to use it for, perhaps a down payment on a new house or maybe you already used it for the honeymoon.

All done! Now, you can relax, because the work of the wedding is over.

MEMORIALIZING
YOUR WEDDING

DECIDE AT YOUR LEISURE how you'd like to memorialize your wedding. You probably have a photographer and a videographer hard at work on an album and a video keepsake, but there are other pieces of your wedding that are still lying around. You don't want to throw them away, but you're not sure what to do with them.

Some ideas:

- Take a shoebox full of pieces to a mosaicist and commission a decorative platter or picture frame. Mosaicists can incorporate text (place cards or invitations), fabric (pieces of the chuppah), pieces of a broken glass from a Jewish ceremony, dried flowers from the bridal bouquets, inedible cake accessories such as Swarovski crystals or silver beads, photographs and pretty much anything else you'd like.

- Keep and display the engraving plate that was used to make your invitations.

- Frame the *ketubah* or marriage license.

- Make a scrapbook as a companion to the photo album with all of your wedding stationery and mementos: the notes you've jotted at the back of

> *SO WE GREW TOGETHER*
> *LIKE TO A DOUBLE CHERRY,*
> *SEEMING PARTED,*
> *BUT YET A UNION IN PARTITION;*
> *TWO LOVELY BERRIES*
> *MOULDED ON ONE STEM.*
> —WILLIAM SHAKESPEARE

this book, save-the-dates, invitations, ceremony programs, place cards, the cards on which you've written your vows. If you've been keeping a planning journal, you can easily turn this into a scrapbook.

If you just can't decide what to do with all the bits and pieces, store them away in a clear plastic container and put off the decision for a later date. Be assured that no matter how you choose to memorialize your wedding day, it'll be an occasion impossible to forget.

NOTES

The greatest happiness is the conviction that we are loved, loved for ourselves, or rather loved in spite of ourselves. —VICTOR HUGO

Love is indescribable and unconditional.
I could tell you a thousand things that it is not,
but not one that it is. —DUKE ELLINGTON

Once upon a time, on a day that looked like any other day, someone like no one else came along and made life into something that would never be the same. —Anonymous

_____

_____

_____

_____

_____

_____

_____

_____

_____

_____

_____

_____

_____

_____

_____

_____

_____

_____

To get the full value of joy, you must have someone to divide it with. —MARK TWAIN

Love is the only flower that grows and blossoms without the aid of seasons. —KAHLIL GIBRAN

INDEX